About this book

This book looks at the natural resources that are found and used around the world. These include essentials, such as water and food, but also natural resources such as metals that make bicycles, mobile phones and other things that we enjoy having can live without.

The location of a country determines natural resources it has and the distribution of these resources affect a country's development. For example, some countries with plenty of mineral resources have developed industries that turn those minerals into products.

There is a limited amount of most of the Earth's natural resources and one day they will run out. Digging up or obtaining these resources can damage or destroy habitats. Also, processing raw materials into products uses large amounts of energy, which causes pollution and contributes to climate change. In the future, it will become increasingly important to find alternative ways of sourcing natural resources, such as recycling.

Each double page in this book introduces the location and distribution of natural resources in a different region of the world. A map locates relevant sites and graphs and statistics provide important data. At the end of the book is a section you can use for further study and comparisons.

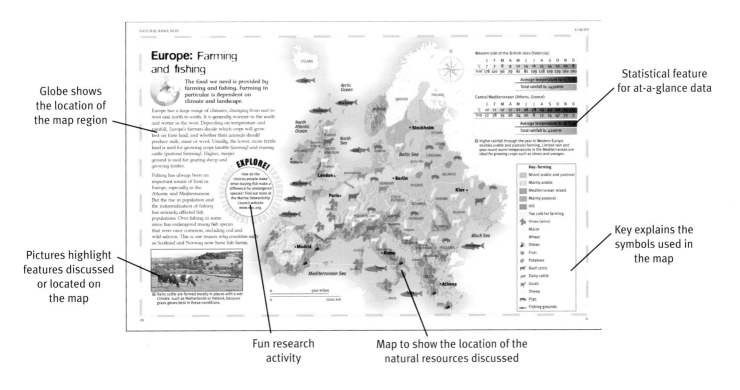

Globe shows the location of the map region

Pictures highlight features discussed or located on the map

Fun research activity

Map to show the location of the natural resources discussed

Statistical feature for at-a-glance data

Key explains the symbols used in the map

The world: Water supply

Water is an essential natural resource. People can survive for three weeks without food, but may die after three days without water. We need water to live, to cook, keep clean, grow crops and raise livestock. People also use water for non-essential purposes. Industrialised countries use vast amounts of water in factories and power stations, and in things like washing machines and swimming pools.

There is a limited, or finite, amount of water on Earth and people in different locations have a different share of it. Water availability is mainly affected by climate. Places with hot, dry climates, such as deserts, have little rainfall. Places with rainy seasons have more water and can store surplus water in reservoirs. In some places water is polluted, so cannot be safely used by people without expensive treatment. With a rising global population, and increasing non-essential water use, supplying enough water for everyone is a major challenge in the 21st century.

NORTH AMERICA

Mojave Desert

Sonoran Desert

SOUTH AMERICA

Atacama Desert

Monte Desert

6 billion
World population

0.5 billion
Chronically short of water

Year 2000

8.9 billion
World population

4 billion
Chronically short of water

Year 2050 (projected)

⬆ By 2050, experts predict that nearly half the world's population will have a chronic water shortage. This means they will not have enough to remain healthy.

NATURAL RESOURCES

Jack and Meg Gillett
With contributions by Richard and Louise Spilsbury

WAYLAND

Contents

The world: Water supply — 4

The world: Fossil fuels — 6

Europe: Metallic minerals — 8

The British Isles: Building materials — 10

Africa: Precious metals and stones — 12

North America: Industrial raw materials — 14

The Poles: Gas and oil — 16

The world: Forests and forest products — 18

Europe: Farming and fishing — 20

South-East Asia: Monoculture — 22

Brazil: Forest and farmland — 24

North America: Extensive farming — 26

Australia: Irrigation farming — 28

Now test yourself! — 30

Glossary — 31

Index — 32

N

ASIA

EUROPE

Gobi Desert

Thar
Desert

Sahara

Arabian
Desert

AFRICA

Kalahari
Desert

Great
Sandy
Desert

AUSTRALASIA

Great
Victoria
Desert

EXPLORE!

Think of all
the ways in which
you use water. Which
of these are essential,
and which are
non-essential?

Key

Areas that usually have a water surplus

Areas that are chronically short of water

The world: Fossil fuels

Coal, gas and oil are natural resources that we call fossil fuels. They formed from the remains of plants and animals that lived millions of years ago. We mostly use these resources to generate useful energy.

Coal is mostly burned in power stations to generate electricity. Gas is also used in power stations, as well as being piped into homes to use for heating and cooking. Petrol and diesel made from oil are essential to make the engines in cars, aeroplanes and ships work. We use enormous amounts of energy and this is rising each year because of the growing world population and increased use of vehicles and electricity in modern life.

Some countries have more fossil fuel reserves than others, but all fossil fuels will run out one day. Another problem is that burning fossil fuels causes pollution. This is why people are looking for alternative, sustainable energy resources, such as water, wind and solar (sun) power.

Greenland

Alaska (USA)

Canada

NORTH AMERICA

USA

Mexico

Venezuela

Colombia

Ecuador

SOUTH AMERICA

Peru

Brazil

Bolivia

Paraguay

Uruguay

Chile

Argentina

Years

300
250
200
150
100
50
0

Coal
Gas
Oil

⬆ This bar graph shows how many years we can still use each fossil fuel (as of 2009).

⬆ Oil refineries changes crude oil from underground into fuels and many other by-products such as plastics.

N

Iceland

Norway
Sweden
Finland

Russian Federation

ASIA

UK

EUROPE Ukraine

France

Kazakhstan

Mongolia

Spain

Turkey

China

Japan

Morocco
Algeria Libya Egypt

Iraq Iran

Saudi
Arabia

Pakistan

India

Key

Oil field

Coalfield

Gas field

Mali

Niger Chad Sudan

Nigeria

Thailand

AFRICA Ethiopia

Malaysia

Dem.
Repub.
of Congo

Angola

Indonesia

Papua
New
Guinea

Zambia

Namibia

Madagascar

Australia

AUSTRALASIA

South
Africa

EXPLORE!

Find out
which of the three
fossil fuels pollutes
the air the most.
Which pollutes the
air the least?

New
Zealand

Antarctica

Europe: Metallic minerals

Metallic minerals are natural substances from the Earth from which we get metals such as copper and iron. These metals are used to produce many of the products we use in everyday life including aeroplanes, bridges and computers.

Different amounts and types of metals are found in rocks called ores in different locations worldwide. The Industrial Revolution began in Europe because of the metallic minerals there. The region also had fossil fuels to power machines and factories that turned the raw materials into products, such as ships and railways.

There is a limited supply of metallic minerals and they are being used up as people buy more and develop new metal products. For example, silver, used for electronics and jewellery, could run out by 2020. We can recycle some metals by melting and reusing them. It takes five tonnes of bauxite ore to make one tonne of new aluminium, but none to make recycled aluminium.

⬆ This steelworks in Sheffield, UK, uses iron ore found nearby to make steel and local coal to power its machines.

EXPLORE!

Find out which metallic minerals are used to produce the following products: mobile phone, car, computer and fridge.

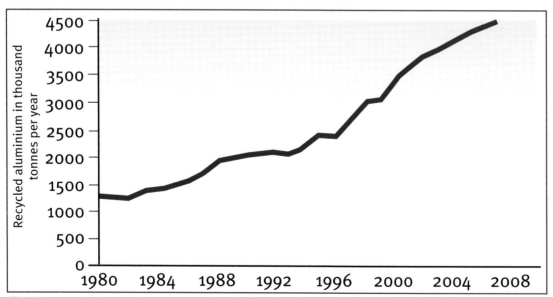

⬆ This graph shows how much aluminium has been recycled in Europe since 1980. The amount is increasing, currently reaching to around 90 per cent of drinks cans. Today, Europe is a global leader in recycling metals along with North America and Japan.

Key

- Coniferous forest
- Mixed farming
- Arable farming, the Great Plains
- Pastoral farming
- Hot desert
- Ice desert
- Vegetable growing on irrigated farmland

See p. 21 for crop and animal symbols key

Arctic Ocean

Great Bear Lake

Northwest Territories

on ritory

Nunavut

Hudson Bay

Labrador

Newfoundland and Labrador

Newfoundland

CANADA

Alberta

Saskatchewan

Lake Athabasca

Great Slave Lake

Manitoba

Lake Manitoba

Lake Winnipeg

Ontario

Québec

St Lawrence

New Brunswick

Nova Scotia

Grand Banks

Rocky Mountains

British Columbia

• Edmonton

• Vancouver

• Saskatoon

• Winnipeg

Montana

North Dakota

Minnesota

Lake Superior

The Great Lakes

Michigan

Lake Huron

Montréal

Ottawa •

New York

Maine

Cod

Herring

Hake

• Seattle

Washington

Oregon

Idaho

Wyoming

South Dakota

USA

Wisconsin

Lake Michigan

Lake Erie

Toronto

Pennsylvania

• Boston

• New York

New Jersey

Sacramento

Nevada

Utah

Colorado

Iowa

Nebraska

• Denver

Chicago •

Indiana

Ohio

West Virginia

Virginia

Washington D.C.

Maryland

Delaware

East States Key
1 New Hampshire
2 Vermont
3 Massachusetts
4 Rhode Island
5 Connecticut

• Las Vegas

California

Arizona

New Mexico

• Phoenix

os Angeles

St. Louis •

Kansas

Missouri

Kentucky

Tennessee

Arkansas

Oklahoma

North Carolina

South Carolina

Georgia

North Atlantic Ocean

Texas

Louisiana

Mississippi

Alabama

• Austin

New Orleans •

Florida

Gulf of Mexico

• Miami

N

0   500 miles

0   1000 km

27

Australia: Irrigation farming

Australia is one of the world's driest countries. Two thirds of its area is classed as arid, with insufficient rainfall for plants to grow, and much of this is barren desert. The hot, arid interior of Australia is only suitable for rearing sheep and cattle where farmers can irrigate the land.

Crops including wheat, barley, sorghum and cotton mostly grow in wetter New South Wales and Victoria, but big, regular harvests can only be guaranteed in most areas using irrigation from both rivers and groundwater. Digging ever deeper for sufficient groundwater is causing widespread salination in Australia. This is when underground salts come to the surface making soil useless for crops or pasture.

When soil damaged by salination, livestock trampling, and pesticide pollution dries up, it can crumble and blow away, so farmland turns to desert. Desertification threatens 70 per cent of Australia's farmland. Sustainable farming and water conservation are vital if agriculture for Australians and for export is to survive into the future.

Ashburton River

Perth•

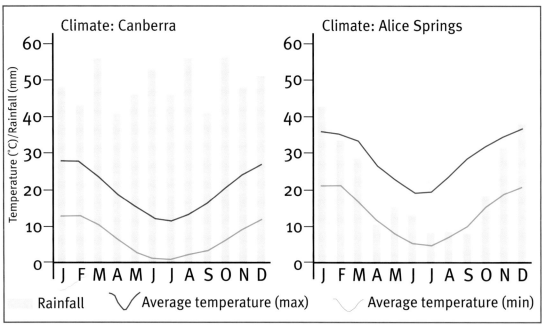

⬆ Coastal Canberra, New South Wales, has rain through the year caused by moist air blown from the ocean, but Alice Springs has a typical arid to desert climate.

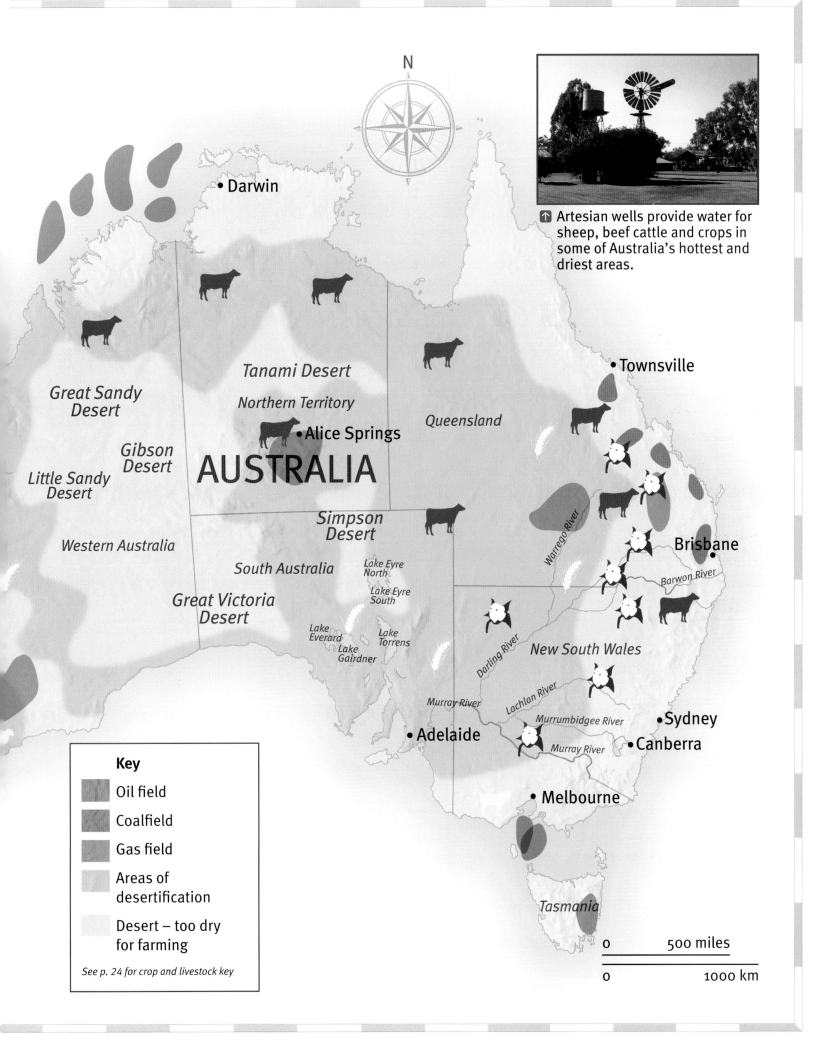

N

Darwin

Artesian wells provide water for sheep, beef cattle and crops in some of Australia's hottest and driest areas.

Townsville

Great Sandy Desert

Tanami Desert

Northern Territory

Queensland

Gibson Desert

Alice Springs

AUSTRALIA

Little Sandy Desert

Brisbane

Warrego River

Barwon River

Western Australia

Simpson Desert

South Australia

Lake Eyre North

Lake Eyre South

Great Victoria Desert

Lake Everard

Lake Gairdner

Lake Torrens

Darling River

New South Wales

Lachlan River

Murray River

Murrumbidgee River

Sydney

Adelaide

Murray River

Canberra

Melbourne

Tasmania

Key

Oil field

Coalfield

Gas field

Areas of desertification

Desert – too dry for farming

See p. 24 for crop and livestock key

0   500 miles

0   1000 km

29

Now test yourself!

These questions will help you to revisit some of the information in this book. To answer the questions, you will need to use the contents on page 2 and the index on page 32, as well as the relevant pages on each topic.

1 Use the contents on page 2 to find which pages show a map of:

(a) Europe's main fishing areas.

(b) the largest farming areas in the USA.

(c) the most southerly place on the Earth's surface.

2 Use the index on page 32 to find the pages which will tell you:

(a) which parts of the world don't have enough water for people to live in.

(b) how paper is made from wood.

(c) how people in Bali can grow rice on steep hillsides.

3 Use the glossary on page 31 to complete a copy of this table:

Key word	Meaning of this word
	The loss of forest due to chopping down large numbers of trees.
Irrigation	
	Rocks that have useful metals in them.
	When people don't have all the water they need.

4 Use page 4 to find out how long people can survive without any food or water.

5 Use page 8 to find out what ores contain.

6 Use page 14 to list any three industrial raw materials and what they are used to make.

7 Use page 28 to find out which farm animal is produced in very large numbers by Australia.

8 Antarctica is a continent, but the Arctic is not. Use pages 16 and 17 to find out why.

9 Which country produces most of the world's:

(a) diamonds?

(b) rice?

(c) tropical hardwoods, such as mahogany?

10 How is the world's increasing population putting pressure on its natural resources?

Glossary

chronic lasting for a long time

climate change any long-term significant changes to the weather pattern of a certain area. Climate change can have natural causes, such as volcano eruptions, and is also the result of global warming.

coniferous an evergreen tree with cones

deciduous a deciduous tree is one that loses its leaves in the autumn

deforestation the loss of forest due to the clearing of large numbers of trees

desertification the word used to describe the spread of the world's deserts

fertile land area with soil that has all the nutrients plants need to grow healthily

finite resources resources which will run out at some time in the future

fossil fuels sources of energy (like coal, oil and gas) formed from plants and animals which died millions of years ago

global warming rising temperatures worldwide, caused by the increase of gases in the air that trap the Sun's heat near the earth.

industrial raw materials natural resources that are used to make goods

irrigation putting extra water onto the soil because there isn't enough rain to grow crops

natural resources materials such as rocks, soil and water which can be used to meet people's needs

ores rocks that have useful metals in them

recycling when waste materials are used again to make new products

sustainability using natural resources in ways which allow people to use them for much longer and cause the least damage to the natural environment

tropical rainforests dense forests which grow in hotter, wetter places nearer to the Equator

water deficit when people don't have all the water they need

water surplus when people have more water than they need

Index

A
Africa 12
Antarctica 16
Arctic Ocean 17
Asia 17, 22
Australia 28

B
Brazil 24
British Isles 10
building materials 10

C
Canada 14, 26
China 22, 24
climate 3, 4, 12, 18, 20, 21, 22, 26, 28
climate change 3, 12
coal 6, 8, 16, 17

D
deforestation 10, 18, 24
desertification 28
deserts 4, 12, 16, 28, 29

E
electricity generation 6

energy 3, 6
Europe 8, 17, 20, 24

F
farming 12, 20, 22, 24, 26, 28
finite resources 4, 6, 16, 17, 18
fishing 16, 20
forests 10, 18, 24, 26
fossil fuels 6, 7, 8, 14, 16, 17

G
gas 6, 16, 17
global warming 17, 18
GM crops 26

I
irrigation 21, 28

M
metals 3, 8, 12, 14, 16, 17
monoculture 22

N
North America 8, 14, 17, 26

O
oil 6, 14, 16, 17
ores 8, 14

P
Poles 16, 17
pollution 3, 4, 6, 7, 16, 17, 22, 28
population growth 4, 6, 20, 24, 26

R
raw materials 3, 8, 10, 14
recycling 3, 8

S
soil 3, 26, 28
South America 24
South-East Asia 22
sustainability 6, 16, 18, 22, 28

T
tropical rainforests 18, 24

U
USA 14, 17, 26

W
water supply 4, 28
whaling 16
world 3, 4, 6, 14, 18, 22, 24, 26

Published in paperback in 2014 by Wayland
Copyright © Wayland 2014

Wayland
Hachette Children's Books
338 Euston Road
London NW1 3BH

Wayland Australia
Level 17/207
Kent Street
Sydney, NSW 2000

All rights reserved.

Editor: Julia Adams
Designer: Rob Walster, Big Blu Design
Cover design: Wayland
Map Art: Martin Sanders
Illustrations: Andy Stagg
Picture research: Kathy Lockley/Julia Adams

The website addresses (URLs) included in this book were valid at the time of going to press. However, it is possible that contents or addresses may have changed since the publication of this book No responsibility for any such changes can be accepted by either the author or the Publisher.

British Library Cataloguing in Publication Data
Gillett, Jack.
 Maps of the environmental world.
 Natural resources.
 1. Natural resources--Juvenile literature. 2. Natural resources--Maps for children.
 I. Title II. Gillett, Meg.
 333.7-dc22

ISBN 978 0 7502 8273 4
Printed in Malaysia
10 9 8 7 6 5 4 3 2 1

Wayland is a division of Hachette Children's Books, an Hachette UK company.
www.hachette.co.uk

Picture acknowledgements:
All photography: Shutterstock, except: p. 10: Jack and Meg Gillett; p. 13, p. 24: iStock Images; p. 17: Paul Andrew Lawrence / Alamy

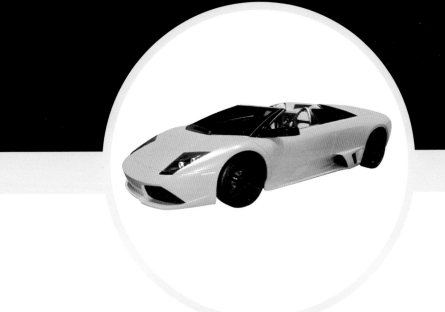

Chris Oxlade

Francis Holland School NW1 6XR

WITHDRAWN

T2154

Raintree is an imprint of Capstone Global Library Limited, a company incorporated in England and Wales having its registered office at 264 Banbury Road, Oxford OX2 7DY – Registered company number: 6695582

www.raintree.co.uk
myorders@raintree.co.uk

Edited by Helen Cox-Cannons
Designed by Philippa Jenkins
Picture research by Svetlana Zhurkin
Production by Steve Walker
Originated by Capstone Global Library Ltd
Printed and bound in India.

ISBN 978 1 4747 4039 5 (hardback)
21 20 19 18 17
10 9 8 7 6 5 4 3 2

ISBN 978 1 4747 4043 2 (paperback)
22 21 20 19 18
10 9 8 7 6 5 4 3 2 1

British Library Cataloguing in Publication Data
A full catalogue record for this book is available from the British Library.

Acknowledgements
We would like to thank the following for permission to reproduce photographs: Alamy: Sueddeutsche Zeitung Photo, 22; Dreamstime: Marilyn Gould, cover (left); iStockphoto: BernardAllum, 12; Library of Congress, 21; NASA, 25, 29; National Geographic Creative: H.M. Herget, 10; Newscom: akg-images, 17, 18, 19, 20, Design Pics, 8, Heritage Images/London Metropolitan Archives, 16, Heritage Images/Werner Forman Archive, 6, Hilary Jane Morgan, 11, Mirrorpix, 15, Mirrorpix/Arthur Sidey, 23, picture-alliance/dpa/ Andrej Sokolow, 28, Polaris/Solar Impulse/Rezo/Jean Revillard, 27, Universal Images Group/G. Dagli Orti/ De Agostini, 9, World History Archive, 13; Shutterstock: Everett Collection, 14, IM_photo, 5, Jeffrey B. Banke, 7, K_Boonnitrod, 4, Michael Shake, 1, Nerthuz, cover (right), Pavel L Photo and Video, 26, wws001, 24.

We would like to thank Matthew Anniss for his help in the preparation of this book.

Contents

Transport then and now 4

Wheels and carts 6

Boats and sailing 8

Trade and discovery 10

Canals and railways 12

Steamships 14

Bikes and motorbikes 16

Cars 18

The first aircraft 20

Bigger and faster planes 22

Space travel 24

New forms of power 26

Future transport 28

Glossary 30

Find out more 31

Index 32

Some words are shown in bold,
like this. You can find out what they
mean by looking in the glossary.

Thousands of years ago, during the Stone Age, most people in the world did not travel far from home. There were no cars or bicycles and no roads. People might have walked along a path to the next village.

People learned to train animals such as yaks to carry packs about 6,000 years ago.

Millions of people fly in aeroplanes every day.

Since the Stone Age, there have been many new inventions. They have made transport easier and faster. We can now travel easily between towns and cities. We can even travel half-way around the world in a day in aeroplanes.

The wheel was invented in about 3500 BC. The first wheels were made of planks joined edge to edge. A simple two-wheeled cart could carry a lot more on it than an animal could carry on its back.

This work of art was made in c.2500 BC. It shows Sumerians using a cart with an early version of wheels.

Cart wheels wore tracks into the stones of this Roman road.

Wheels with **spokes** were invented in about 2000 BC. Spoked wheels were lighter and stronger than solid wheels. Hundreds of years later, the ancient Romans began building roads paved with stone. This made travel across their huge **empire** easier.

People may have gone to sea on rafts made from logs or **reeds** as long as 40,000 years ago. The oldest boats ever found are from around 10,000 years ago. They were dug-out canoes made out of tree trunks.

Dug-out canoes were made by burning away wood to make a hollow.

Egyptian boats had sails made from **papyrus** or **linen**.

People simply paddled their boats until sails were invented in about 3100 BC. The first known sailing boats travelled on the River Nile in Egypt. Their square sails were raised up to catch the wind.

Around the world, craftsmen slowly learned how to build bigger, stronger and faster ships. Most ships had a **hull** of wooden planks over a wooden frame. **Cargo** such as **grain**, wine and oil were loaded on board.

The ancient Greeks traded goods around their empire.

A **carrack** was a ship that sailed around Europe during the 14th century.

Explorers sailed across the oceans to explore new land. Some went to claim new land as their own. New inventions such as the **rudder** made long journeys by sea much easier.

During the 1800s, engineers in Europe and the United States dug hundreds of kilometres of canals. Barges carried **cargo** such as coal or dry foods along the canals between cities, ports and factories. A barge could carry more than a wagon on a road.

This illustration from 1828 shows barges carrying cargo along a London canal.

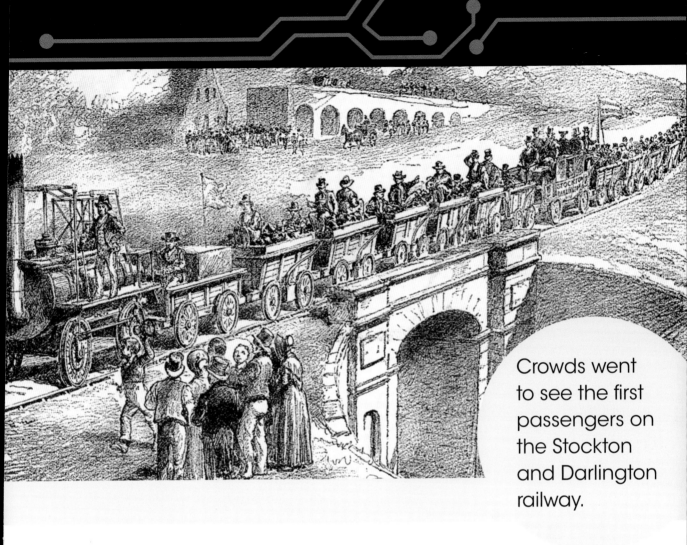

Crowds went to see the first passengers on the Stockton and Darlington railway.

In 1825, the world's first passenger railway started running. It was called the Stockton and Darlington Railway. Passenger coaches were pulled along by horses, then later by steam-powered **locomotives**. The first underground railway opened in London in 1863.

By the end of the 1700s, steam-powered ships began to take over from sailing ships. Steam engines turned paddle wheels or propellers in the water. Steamships were easily faster than sailing ships because they did not need wind to power them.

In 1819 *Savannah* became the first steamship to cross the Atlantic Ocean.

paddle wheel

French liner
SS *Normandie*
was the fastest
liner of its time.

Shipbuilders began building steamships
with metal instead of wood. By the 1930s, huge
steam-powered liners were carrying people
around the world. The biggest and fastest liners
sailed across the Atlantic Ocean between
Europe and the United States.

In 1817, German engineer Karl Drais invented a heavy wooden bicycle with no pedals. It was known as a *draisienne*. In 1885, the first modern-looking bicycle was built. It was the Rover Safety bicycle.

A rider moved a *draisienne* along by pushing his or her feet against the ground.

Daimler's motorcycle was the first in the world.

In 1869, Frenchman Ernest Michaux put a small steam engine on a bicycle. Then, in 1885, Gottlieb Daimler built a motorcycle with a petrol engine. Within a few years, motorcycles were popular across Europe and the United States.

The word "car" possibly comes from the Romans. The Latin word *carrus* means "wheeled vehicle". The first cars of the 1800s were horse-drawn carriages with engines. German inventors Karl Benz and Gottlieb Daimler built two of the very first cars in 1885 and 1886.

Karl Benz built this car in 1885.

Ford built a special factory to build the Model T car.

Before long, there were lots of small car-making factories. But these cars were very expensive. Then, in 1908, the American company Ford started making their Model T car. It was small, cheap and easy to look after.

In 1783, a human took off in a flying machine for the first time. The machine was a hot-air balloon. It was built in France by the Montgolfier brothers. About 100 years later, people began to travel in giant gas-filled airships.

Between 1928 and 1937, the Graf Zeppelin airship took thousands of people across the Atlantic Ocean.

Orville was the pilot of the *Flyer's* 12-second flight. Wilbur ran along beside it.

American brothers Orville and Wilbur Wright made history in 1903. They built the first successful powered aeroplane. It was called the *Flyer*. The *Flyer's* first flight lasted just 12 seconds. Many other inventors soon took to the air.

By the end of World War I (1914–1918), there were large bomber aircraft. Some of these bombers were turned into planes to carry passengers. These were the first airliners. Airliners got larger, faster and more comfortable through the 1920s and 1930s.

The Boeing 314 Clipper was a flying boat that landed on water.

The giant Boeing 747 airliner made its first flight in 1970.

The jet engine was a very important invention in the history of air transport. It allowed aircraft to fly much faster and higher than before. The first jet fighter planes flew in 1939. By the 1950s, big jet airliners were taking off.

Rockets are machines that transport spacecraft into space. Rockets were developed in the 1920s and 1930s. By the 1960s, rockets were carrying astronauts on board spacecraft into space.

Soviet **cosmonaut** Yuri Gagarin went into space in 1961, on board a Vostok spacecraft.

Armstrong and Aldrin landed on the Moon in this lunar module.

In 1969, two American astronauts, Neil Armstrong and Buzz Aldrin, landed on the Moon. They travelled there with Michael Collins in the Apollo 11 spacecraft. Another spacecraft, the *Space Shuttle*, made dozens of trips to space between 1981 and 2011.

Types of fuel in engines include petrol and **diesel**. These engines give out gases that **pollute** the air. In the 1990s, **hybrid** cars and electric cars were developed. Electric cars do not pollute the air.

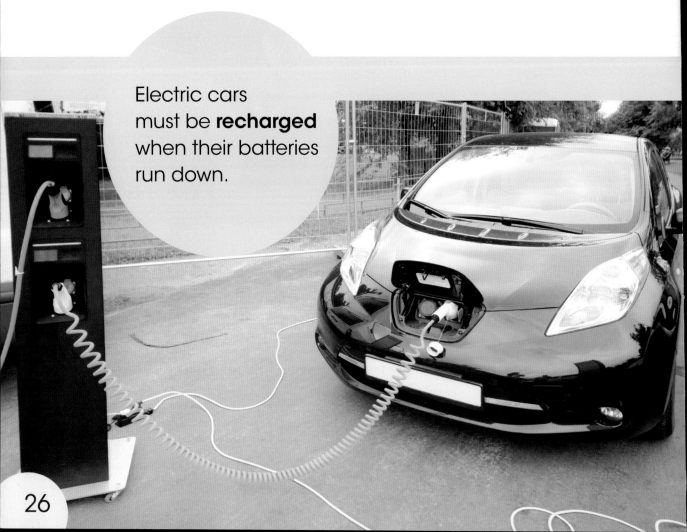

Electric cars must be **recharged** when their batteries run down.

Solar Impulse 2 is a solar-powered plane. It flew all the way around the world in 2016.

Engineers are now making solar-powered cars, boats and planes. This means they have solar panels that capture light from the Sun. The vehicles then turn the light into electricity to power their electric motors.

What new forms of transport will we see in the near future? Driverless cars are already being tested and driverless taxis are being used in Pittsburgh, USA. The car drives itself. It finds its own way from place to place by computer. We could all be using driverless cars one day.

This is a driverless car being tested by Google.

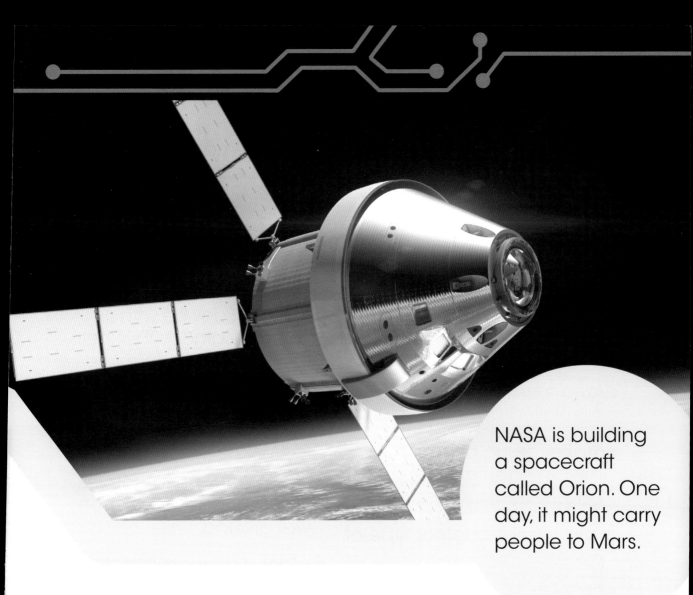

NASA is building a spacecraft called Orion. One day, it might carry people to Mars.

In the air, **drones** and giant airships may start carrying **cargo**. Engineers are designing new spacecraft. They hope these spacecraft will one day carry astronauts and all their food and equipment to Mars.

cargo goods carried on a ship or other vehicle

carrack medieval sailing ship with three or four masts

cosmonaut Russian astronaut

diesel type of fuel used in many vehicle engines

drone unmanned, remote-controlled aircraft

empire group of countries ruled by a single person or government

grain wheat, or other type of cereal

hull main body of a ship, which makes it float

hybrid car that has both an electric motor and an engine that uses fuel

linen type of cloth similar to cotton

locomotive railway engine

papyrus material made from papyrus, which is a water plant

pollute put harmful or dangerous chemicals into the environment

propeller device with spinning blades that help a ship or aeroplane move

recharge to put electricity into a battery, so the battery can be used again

reed plant with tall leaves that grows in water or on wet ground

rudder flat handle at the back of a boat used for steering

spoke rod that joins the centre of a wheel to the rim of a wheel

Books

Cars, Trains, Ships and Planes (Dorling Kindersley, 2015)

Getting Around Through the Years: How Transport Has Changed in Living Memory, Clare Lewis (Raintree, 2016)

The Wright Brothers, Helen Cox Cannons (Raintree, 2016)

Websites

Learn all about travel and transport at this BBC learning site:
http://www.bbc.co.uk/education/topics/zs9k7ty/resources/1

This excellent web page shows the history of cars:
http://www.dkfindout.com/uk/transport/history-cars/

This web page shows a timeline of the history of the bicycle:
http://www.icebike.org/58-milestones-from-bicycle-history-you-must-know/

Index

aeroplanes 5, 21, 22–23
airships 20

barges 12
Benz, Karl 18
bicycles 16, 17
boats 8–9
bomber aircraft 22

canals 12
carts 6–7
cars 18–19

driverless cars 28
driverless taxis 28

electric cars 26
engines 26–27
   solar-powered cars 27
Daimler, Gottlieb 17, 18
Drais, Karl 16

hot-air balloons 20

Michaux, Ernest 17
Montgolfier brothers 20
motorcycles 17

railways 13

sailing 8–9, 10, 11, 14
space travel 24–25
   lunar module 25
   Moon landing 25
   rockets 24
   spacecraft 24, 25, 29
Space Shuttle 25
steamships 14–15

wheels 6–7
Wright brothers 21